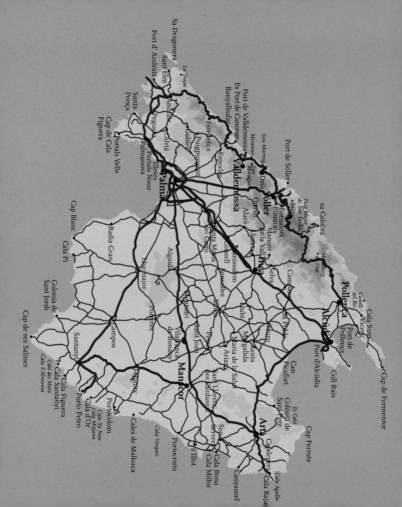

MALLORCA

● Resplendent as a gem under the Mediterranean sun, Spain's largest island, Mallorca forms part of the Balearic Islands archipelago, approximately 200 km from the mainland. Mallorca is an island of great wealth – its riches lying in both the island's cultural heritage and the land's extraordinary natural splendour. At only 3 640 km², this little paradise offers such diversity and charisma, that it has enchanted mankind for centuries.

● Resplandeciente cual gema bajo el sol mediterráneo, Mallorca forma parte del archipiélago de las Islas Baleares. Aproximadamente a 200 km de la península, Mallorca es una isla de gran riqueza: sus tesoros se encuentran tanto en el patrimonio cultural como en el extraordinario esplendor natural de la tierra. Con sólo 3 640 km², este pequeño paraíso ofrece tal diversidad y carisma que ha encantado a la humanidad durante siglos.

● Prächtig wie ein Edelstein, so fügt sich Mallorca, Spaniens größte Insel, ein in den Archipel der Balearen, in einer Entfernung von ungefähr 200 km vom spanischen Festland. Mallorca ist eine Insel von großem Reichtum - reich sowohl an kulturellem Erbe als auch an Natur und Landschaft. Trotz seiner eher geringen Fläche von nur 3 640 km² verfügt dieses kleine Paradies über eine solche Vielfalt und Anziehungskraft, dass es die Menschheit bereits seit Jahrhunderten in seinen Bann zu ziehen vermag.

● Palma de Mallorca is the island's capital, a bustling marine metropolis that beats to a lively tune. Tree-fringed streets give way to spacious squares where outdoor café's and restaurants entice and delight. Vessels rock lazily in the azure port under the watchful gaze of the magnificent Palma Cathedral, the city's most famous landmark.

● Palma de Mallorca es la capital de la isla, una pequeña y animada ciudad costera que palpita al son de una alegre melodía. Las calles bordeadas de árboles abren paso a extensas plazas donde las terrazas de los cafés y restaurantes atraen y deleitan al visitante. Los barcos se mecen en el puerto azul celeste bajo la atenta mirada de la espléndida Catedral de Palma, el monumento más famoso de la ciudad.

● Palma de Mallorca, die Hauptstadt der Insel, ist eine lebhafte, kleine Küstenmetropole, geprägt von der lebhaften Melodie des Mittelmeers. Baumgesäumte Straßen führen hin zu großzügigen Plätzen, auf denen Cafés und Restaurants ihren Charme entfalten und zum Verweilen verführen. Schiffe wiegen sich gemächlich im azurblauen Wasser des Hafens unter dem aufmerksamen Blick der prächtigen Kathedrale von Palma, dem berühmtesten Wahrzeichen der Stadt.

● The quaint old town of Palma is a jumble of narrow winding cobblestone streets, and elegant façades of ancient buildings reveal hidden courtyards, all of which characterize the charming ambience of Palma de Mallorca.

● El pintoresco casco viejo de la ciudad es una mezcla de estrechas calles adoquinadas llenas de curvas y elegantes fachadas de antiguos edificios que revelan patios ocultos, todo caracterizado por el encantador ambiente de Palma de Mallorca.

● Die malerische Altstadt von Palma ist ein Wirrwar aus engen, gewundenen Kopfsteinpflastergassen, und hinter eleganten Fassaden der historischen Gebäude kommen versteckte Innenhöfe zum Vorschein: all dies ist charakteristisch für den anmutigen Charme Palma de Mallorcas.

• Mallorca's lengthy history of invasion has left a legacy of architectural diversity. Palma attests to this eclectic fusion of styles, with myriad of influences over the centuries, from the Roman's paved streets, to the fanciful arches of the Moors, lofty Christian Cathedrals, and today's modern apartments.

• Las numerosas invasiones de Mallorca han dejado un legado de diversidad arquitectónica sin igual. Palma es testimonio de esta ecléctica fusión de estilos, con miles de influencias seculares, desde calles adoquinadas por los romanos, hasta los extravagantes arcos árabes, la majestuosa catedral cristiana y los modernos edificios de hoy en día.

• Mallorcas lange, an Invasionen reiche Geschichte brachte ein reiches architektonisches Erbe hervor. In Palma findet dieses im vielfältigen Miteinander der unterschiedlichen Stile und Einflüsse verschiedener Epochen Ausdruck: von den Pflasterstraßen römischen Ursprungs über die verspielten Bögen der Mauren und kühnen christlichen Kathedralen bis zu den modernen Wohnhäusern von heute.

CALA SA NAU

● The south and south-east coast of Mallorca is characterized by its cloudless blue skies, and scorching summer temperatures, but the beauty of this area belongs to the generous amount of coves and inlets with their shallow waters sparkling like turquoise gems.

● La costa sudoeste de Mallorca se caracteriza por sus azules cielos despejados y sus abrasadoras temperaturas veraniegas, pero la belleza de este paraje reside en la generosa cantidad de calias y ensenadas con aguas poco profundas que relucen como gemas.

CALA BELTRAN

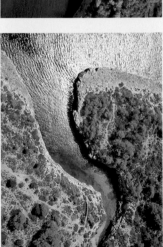

● Wenn auch für die Südwestküste Mallorcas vor allem der wolkenlos blaue Himmel und die Hitze des Sommers charakteristisch sind, so verdankt diese Region ihre Schönheit doch der Vielzahl von Buchten und Zuflüssen, in denen flaches Wasser türkis glitzert als sei es voll von Edelsteinen.

CALA PI

CALÓ DES MORO

● Cala Figuera, along the south-east coast, the sea in this little fishing village extends like a Norwegian fiord into the land. The fish market still retains its atmosphere of days gone by, making this village a popular subject for local painters who are intent on capturing the old Mallorcan charm.

● Cala Figuera: a lo largo de la costa sudeste de esta pequeña aldea de pescadores, el mar se extiende como un fiordo noruego en la tierra. La lonja aún conserva la atmósfera de los días pasados, convirtiendo a esta aldea en un popular paraje para los pintores locales que intentan capturar el encanto de la vieja Mallorca.

● Cala Figuera an der Südostküste – das Meer erstreckt sich in dieses kleine Fischerdorf wie ein norwegischer Fjord. Der Fischmarkt bewahrt bis heute die Atmosphäre vergangener Tage, so dass dieses Dorf ein beliebtes Motiv für die einheimischen Maler darstellt, die in ihren Bildern den Charme des alten Mallorca einfangen möchten.

CALA S'ALMUNIA

CALÓ DES MORO

● White sandy coves, crystal clear waters of an azure blue, bright sunny skies and happy holiday makers are what typify this region of the island. This undulating coast ripples and rolls, revealing many heavenly beaches and inlets where small yachts moor lazily for days.

● Calas de arena blanca, cristalinas aguas azul celeste y brillantes cielos soleados es lo que caracteriza a esta región de la isla. Su costa ondulante se riza y extiende, dando lugar a numerosas playas y paradisíacas ensenadas en las que se mecen perezosamente pequeños yates durante días.

● Weiße Sandbuchten, kristallklares Wasser von azurnem Blau, klarer sonniger Himmel und fröhliche Urlauber sind es, die diese Region der Insel prägen. Entlang der gewundenen Küstenlinie finden sich viele himmlische Strände und natürliche Häfen, in denen schläfrig kleine Jachten liegen.

CALA S'ALMUNIA

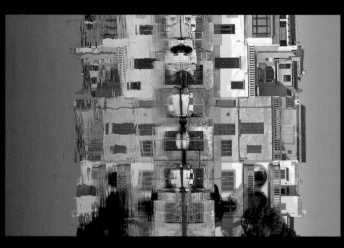

● Portocolom is one of several places in the world that claims to be the birthplace of Christopher Columbus, along with the town of Felanitx just a few kilometres inland. Whatever the case, it's nevertheless a very charming fishing village, established around an attractive natural harbour.

● Portocolom, junto a la ciudad de Felanitx a pocos kilómetros hacia el interior, es uno de los lugares del mundo que alega ser cuna de Cristóbal Colón. No obstante, sea cual fuere el caso, es una aldea pesquera sumamente encantadora, establecida alrededor de un atractivo puerto natural.

Portocolom ist einer von mehreren Orten auf der Welt, die von sich behaupten, der Geburtsort von Christoph Kolumbus zu sein, zusammen mit Felanitx, einer Stadt einige Kilometer landeinwärts. Wahr oder nicht, in jedem Fall handelt es sich um ein sehr anziehendes Fischerdorf, das an einem malerischen natürlichen Hafen gelegen ist.

CALA MONDRAGÓ

CALA VARQUES

- Every so often, there's a beach which is tucked away between cliffs and therefore not that easy to access. These hidden coves have remained untainted, with shimmering warm waters in an inviting aqua-marine palette, and pristine soft white sand, making these inlets veritable treasures.

- De vez en cuando, encontramos playas enclavadas entre acantilados y, por lo tanto, no son de fácil acceso. Estas calas ocultas han permanecido vírgenes, con aguas relucientes y cálidas de una atractiva gama aguamarina, y suaves arenas inmaculadas, que transforman a estas ensenadas en auténticos tesoros.

Von Zeit zu Zeit findet man Strände, die versteckt zwischen den Felsen der Küste liegen und daher schwer zugänglich sind. Diese entlegenen Buchten sind unberührt geblieben, und mit dem warmem Wasser, das in allen Farben des Mittelmeers schimmert, und dem weiß... weichen Sand sind sie wahre Schätze der Natur

CASTELL DE SANTUERI

● Villages, castles and ruins along the east coast of Mallorca are tell-tale reminders of an ancient past, such as the fortress of Santueri which was reconstructed by the leaders of every age.

● A lo largo de la costa este de Mallorca encontramos aldeas, castillos y ruinas. Son recordatorios que revelan un pasado antiquísimo, como la fortaleza de Santueri, reconstruida en diferentes épocas.

● Die Dörfer, Burgen und Ruinen an der Ostküste Mallorcas sind beredte Zeugen einer lang vergangenen Zeit – so die Festung Santueri, die von den Herrschern der verschiedenen Epochen immer wieder aufgebaut wurde.

CALA AGULLA

● The idyllic and pristine cove of Calla Agulla is the most popular beach in the municipal area of Capdepera, while Es Caló further north, forms part of the municipality of Artà, and environmentalists deem this stretch of coastline to be of great importance.

● La cala idílica e inmaculada de Cala Agulla es la playa más popular del área municipal de Capdepera, mientras que Es Caló, más al norte, forma parte del municipio de Artà. Los ecologistas consideran este tramo de costa de gran importancia biológica.

● Die idyllische und naturbelassene Bucht von Cala Agulla ist der beliebteste Strand in der Gegend von Capdepera, während Es Caló weiter nördlich zum Verwaltungsgebiet von Artà gehört. Ökologen messen diesem Küstenbereich große Bedeutung bei.

● The name of this town comes from the Arabic al-kudia, meaning hill, which aptly describes its location, characterizing the town is a beautiful Roman open-air amphitheatre, and the 13th century Gothic church of Sant Jaume.

● El nombre de este pueblo viene del árabe "alkudia", que significa colina, y describe a la perfección esta ubicación. Lo que caracteriza al pueblo es el pequeño anfiteatro romano al aire libre, la iglesia gótica de Sant Jaume del siglo XIII y especialmente su espléndida muralla medieval.

● Der Name dieser Stadt geht auf das Arabische al-kudia (Hügel) zurück, eine Bezeichnung, die durchaus treffend ihre Lage beschreibt. Kennzeichnend für die Stadt ist ein schönes Freiluft-Amphitheater aus römischer Zeit sowie die gotische Kirche Sant Jaume aus dem 13. Jahrhundert.

COLL BAIX

- Nestled between two tall cliffs, the beach of Coll Baix is the only beach in the area that has been left as nature intended – beautifully wild and unspoilt.

- Enclavada entre dos altos acantilados, la playa de Coll Baix es la única de la zona que se ha dejado a merced de la naturaleza: deliciosamente agreste y virgen.

- Eingepasst zwischen zwei hohen Klippen ist der Strand von Coll Baix, der einzige Strand des Gebiets, der so belassen wurde, wie die Natur ihn schuf – wunderbar wild und unverfälscht.

● At the northernmost point of the island, is Cap de Formentor, a peninsula that stretches approximately 20 km out to sea, its precipitous cliffs plummeting from as high as 400 metres into the sea. At the point where the lighthouse stands there are spectacular views for miles around.

● En el punto más septentrional de la isla se encuentra Cap de Formentor, una península que se extiende aproximadamente unos 20 km hacia el mar. Sus acantilados escarpados tienen una caída brusca de hasta 400 metros de altura. En el extremo, el faro ofrece unas vistas espectaculares.

● An der nördlichsten Spitze der Insel liegt Cap de Formentor, eine Halbinsel, die sich ungefähr 20 km in das Meer erstreckt. Seine steilen Klippen stürzen sich aus einer Höhe von bis zu 400 Metern in die See. Auf der Spitze bietet ein Leuchtturm eine atemberaubende, kilometerweite Aussicht.

● Cala Figuera de Pollença is one of three 'Cala Figuera' coves in Mallorca, the others are in Calvià and Santanyí. The road that snakes its way to the tip of Cap de Formentor, offers some of the most spectacular views of this cove.

● Cala Figuera de Pollença es una de las tres calas llamadas 'Cala Figuera' de Mallorca; las otras se encuentran en Calvià y Santanyí. El camino que serpentea hacia el extremo de Cap de Formentor ofrece algunas de las vistas más espectaculares de esta cala.

● Cala Figuera de Pollença ist eine von drei Buchten mit dem Namen „Cala Figuera" auf Mallorca – die anderen sind in Calvià und Santanyí. Die Straße, die sich zum Cap de Formentor schlängelt, bietet einige der spektakulärsten Anblicke der Bucht.

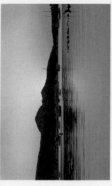

● Built by the Romans, the original coastal town of Pollentia was vulnerable and was completely decimated in 456. The few Romans who survived rebuilt Pollentia 5km inland, and it later became known as Pollença. Its famous landmark is the staircase that climbs Calvari Hill.

● Construida por los romanos, la original ciudad costera de Pollentia era vulnerable y fue completamente diezmada en el año 456. Los romanos que sobrevivieron construyeron una nueva Pollentia 5 km tierra adentro, que más tarde se conoció como Pollença. La escalera que asciende al cerro del Calvario es su patrimonio más conocido.

● Die ursprünglich von den Römern erbaute Küstenstadt Pollentia war unzureichend geschützt und wurde im Jahre 456 komplett ausgelöscht. Die wenigen überlebenden Römer gründeten das neue Pollentia 5 km landeinwärts, das später Pollença genannt wurde. Ein berühmtes Wahrzeichen ist die Treppe auf den Kalvarienberg.

● Surrounding Pollença are typical Mallorcian farmlands, and along the coast are a few secluded coves surrounded by striking sheer cliffs and wild landscape. One such cove is the quaint fishing village of Cala Sant Vicenç.

● Alrededor de Pollença se encuentran las típicas tierras de labranza mallorquinas, y a lo largo de la costa hay algunas calas apartadas rodeadas de sorprendentes acantilados escarpados y paisaje agreste. Una de dichas calas es la pintoresca Cala Sant Vicenç.

● Das Umland von Pollença zeigt das für Mallorca typische Ackerland, und an der Küste befinden sich einige abgeschiedene Buchten, umgeben von steilen, schroffen Klippen und herber Landschaft. In einer dieser Buchten liegt Cala Sant Vicenç, ein malerisches Fischerdorf.

● The dramatic bay of Sa Calobra is surrounded by serrated walls of rock climbing to several hundred metres in height on either side of the Torrent de Pareis, originating from two streams – the Gorg Blau and Lluc.

● La espectacular bahía de Sa Calobra está rodeada por paredes de rocas dentadas que se elevan a varios cientos de metros de altura a ambos lados del Torrent de Pareis, que recoge las aguas de dos arroyos: el Torrent de Lluc y el Gorg Blau.

● Die spektakuläre Meeresbucht von Sa Calobra wird begrenzt von den gezackten Wänden der Felsen, die sich zu einigen hundert Metern beiderseits des Torrent de Pareis erheben, des Zwillingsstroms – aus Torrent des Gorg Blau und Torrent de Lluc.

• The north-west of Mallorca is dominated by mountainous terrain known as the Serra de Tramuntana. With the highest rainfall on the island and natural reservoirs, this area is always lush. The peaks of Puig Major, Teix, Massanella and Tomir are coated with snow during winter.

• El noroeste de Mallorca está dominado por una cordillera, conocida como Serra de Tramuntana. Con las precipitaciones más altas de la isla y varias reservas naturales, este área siempre resulta exuberante. Los picos de Puig Major, Teix, Massanella y Tomir están cubiertos de nieve durante algunos inviernos.

• Der Nordwesten Mallorcas ist von bergigem Terrain geprägt, das als Serra de Tramunata bekannt ist. Dieses Gebiet ist sehr fruchtbar und weist die höchste Niederschlagsmenge der Insel auf. Die Gipfel des Puig Major, Teix, Massanella und Tomir sind im Winter schneebedeckt.

BINIARAIX

BINIARAIX

FORNALUTX

FORNALUTX

FORNALUTX

● Only a few miles apart, the quaint towns of Fornalutx and Biniaraix lie on the fertile slopes of the valley of Sóller. Narrow cobbled streets and rustic homes of natural stone typify these picturesque towns, but it is Fornalutx that often wins the prize for being Spain's prettiest village.

● A sólo unos pocos kilómetros, se ubican los pintorescos pueblos de Fornalutx y Biniaraix, en las laderas fértiles del valle de Sóller. Estrechas calles adoquinadas y casas de piedra caracterizan estos pueblos pintorescos, pero es Fornalutx el que destaca por ser considerado el pueblo más bonito de España.

● Nur wenige Kilometer entfernt liegen die malerischen Städte Fornalutx und Biniaraix auf den fruchtbaren Hängen des Tales der Stadt Sóller. Gewundene Kopfsteinpflasterstraßen und ländliche Steinhäuser kennzeichnen jede dieser pittoresken Städte, doch ist es Fornalutx, das oft als schönster Ort Spaniens ausgezeichnet wird.

PORT DE SÓLLER

● Named Sulliar meaning 'gold' by the Moors, because of the golden olive oil originally cultivated here, Sóller has for hundreds of years been famous for its oranges. The last tram in Mallorca, in operation since 1913, still travels the 5 km between the Port and the town of Sóller.

● Denominada originalmente "Sulliar" que significa 'oro' en árabe, debido al aceite de oliva que se cultiva allí, Sóller ha sido también durante siglos famosa por sus naranjas. El último tranvía de Mallorca –en funcionamiento desde 1913– recorre los 5 km que distan entre el puerto y el pueblo de Sóller.

● Sóller, das die Mauren nach der Farbe des hier erzeugten Olivenöls sulliar (Gold) nannten, ist seit Hunderten von Jahren berühmt für seine Orangen. Die letzte Bahnlinie Mallorcas, in Betrieb seit 1913, verbindet die Stadt mit dem 5 km entfernten Hafen.

SANTA MARIA

ALARÓ

ALARÓ CASTLE

● Nestled in and below the mountainous region of the Serra de Tramuntana, Orient, Alaro and Santa Maria are situated on some of the most fertile land of the island. They exude a rural, country charm and tranquility.

● Enclavados tierra adentro, en de la región montañosa de Serra de Tramuntana, Alaró y Santa María son tres poblaciones situadas en algunas de las tierras más fértiles de la isla. La tranquilidad rige sobre ellas e irradian un genuino encanto rural.

● Landeinwärts hinter dem bergigen Gebiet der Serra de Tramuntana befinden sich die Dörfchen Orient und Alaró sowie die Stadt Santa Maria in einer der fruchtbarsten Regionen der Insel. Stille liegt über ihnen, und sie strahlen einen ländlichen, dörflichen Charme aus.

● Deià village took shape from the 10th to the 13th centuries, when the Moors built the terraces and irrigation systems that gave the area its unique quality and agricultural richness. Not far is Cala Deià, an exquisite little shingle beach in a round cove.

● La aldea de Deià se formó entre los siglos X y XIII, cuando los árabes construyeron las terrazas y sistemas de irrigación que dieron al área su riqueza agrícola y calidad característica. La Cala Deià no se encuentra muy lejos del pueblo, es una playa pequeña y exquisita con guijarros.

● Das Dorf Deià entstand im Zeitraum vom 10. bis zum 13. Jahrhundert, als die Mauren das Terrassen- und Bewässerungssystem bauten, dem dieses Gebiet seine Einzigartigkeit und seinen landwirtschaftlichen Reichtum verdankt. Nicht weit davon entfernt ist Cala Deià, ein außergewöhnlicher kleiner Kiesstrand in einer runden Bucht.

MIRAMAR

SON MORAGUES

● A number of magnificent mansions built during the 18th century retain their splendour, due largely to the incredible conservationist methods of Archduke Luis Salvador who eventually owned 1 700 hectares of the island.

● Algunos imponentes edificios, construidos durante el siglo XVIII, conservan aún su esplendor, en gran medida gracias a los estuerzos del Archiduque Luis Salvador, quien llegó incluso a ser propietario de 1 700 hectáreas con el fin de preservarlos.

● Viele der eindrucksvollen Gebäude aus dem 18. Jahrhundert konnten ihre ursprüngliche Pracht bis heute bewahren, nicht zuletzt dank der großartigen Instandhaltungsmaßnahmen des Erzherzogs Luis Salvador, der schließlich 1 700 ha der Insel besaß.

● A golden church spire reaches heavenwards, and below rustic stone buildings lie amongst the greenery in the enchanting village of Valldemossa, made famous by the writer George Sand and her lover Chopin who resided here one winter.

● La aguja de una iglesia dorada se eleva hacia el cielo y, debajo, los rústicos edificios de piedra se extienden entre la vegetación formando el encantador pueblo de Valldemossa, famoso gracias a la escritora George Sand y a su amante, Chopin, que vivieron aquí un invierno.

● Eine goldene Kirchturmspitze strebt gen Himmel, und unter ihr liegen beschauliche Steinhäuser im Grün des bezaubernden Dorfes Valldemossa, das durch die Schriftstellerin George Sand und ihren Liebhaber Frederic Chopin bekannt geworden ist, die hier einen Winter verbrachten.

MIRADOR DE SES ÀNIMES

● The terraced gardens of Banyalbufar, considered to be the landscaping of the Moors, descend towards the Mediterranean below like the ever-expanding 'ripples of a lake.

● Los cultivos en terraza de Banyalbufar, de origen árabe, descienden hacia el Mediterráneo bajando como las ondas de un lago en constante expansión.

● Die Terrassenanlage der Gärten von Banyalbufar, das maurischen Landschaftsarchitekten zugeschrieben wird, läuft wie eine sich endlos in einem stillen See ausbreitende Kräuselung zum Mittelmeer herab.

LA TRAPA

SANT ELM

● Seen from La Trapa and across the waters from Sant Elm, the isle of sa Dragonera was appropriately named because of its dragon-like silhouette.

● Vista desde La Trapa o desde Sant Elm, la isla de Sa Dragonera hace honor a su nombre. Su forma similar a la de un dragón es evidente.

● Von Le Trapa aus betrachtet, über das Meer bei Sant Elm, erkennt man, dass die Insel Dragonera aufgrund ihrer drachenförmigen Silhouette diesen Namen zu Recht bekommen hat.

A DRAGONERA

● Having a reputation as being one of the prettiest harbours in the Mediterranean, Port d'Andratx is also a very busy port due to its large size.

● Al tener la reputación de ser uno de los puertos más bonitos del Mediterráneo y debido a su gran tamaño, Port d'Andratx también es un sitio muy concurrido.

● Port d'Andratx, das als einer der schönsten Häfen des Mittelmeers gilt, ist aufgrund seiner Größe auch einer der geschäftigsten Häfen des Gebiets.

CALA MARMASSEM

● This coastline is notably generous in its amount of inlets and picturesque little bays, where thousands of tourists take advantage of the glorious beaches. Due to this it has seen an extensive amount of development with miles of high-rise hotels, bustling restaurants and nightclubs.

● Esta costa es notablemente generosa en ensenadas y pequeñas calas pintorescas, donde miles de turistas disfrutan de sus playas. Debido a esto, han proliferado centenares de hoteles, restaurantes y animados clubes nocturnos.

● Die Küste geizt nicht mit malerischen Buchten und pittoresken Stellen, an denen Tausende von Touristen sich an den wunderbaren Stränden erfreuen können. Deshalb hat diese Küstenregion eine intensive Entwicklung durchlaufen, mit langen Bereichen mehrstöckiger Hotels, betriebsamen Restaurants und Nachtclubs.

● Whether you find her beauty at a sheltered
cove of turquoise water, down a narrow street
of golden cobble stone, or under the dappled
shade of a gnarled old olive tree, Mallorca will
hold your heart forever.

● Ya sea porque su belleza se encuentre en una
cala protegida de aguas turquesa, en una calle
estrecha de adoquines dorados o bajo la sombra
veteada de un viejo olivo retorcido, Mallorca
le robará el corazón para siempre.

● Ob Sie nun seine Schönheit in Form einer
geschützten Bucht mit türkisfarbenem Wasser,
im Gold einer seiner engen kopfsteingepflasterten
Gässchen oder unter dem fransigen Schatten
der knorrigen Olivenbäume finden: Mallorca wird
Ihnen in unvergesslicher Erinnerung bleiben.

Published by Neil Austen in collaboration with Triangle Postals S.L.

ISBN 978-84-8478-434-0 DL: ME-566/2015

- Photography ● Fotografía ● Aufnahmen: **Neil Austen**
- Text: **Andrea Florens**
- Design by ● Diseño por ● Designed by: **Jeannie Mather**